The Psalms of Solomon

Sacred Songs of Faith and Hope

A Modern Translation

Adapted for the Contemporary Reader

Jewish Scribes
(Intertestamental Period)

Translated by Tim Zengerink

© **Copyright 2025**
All rights reserved.

It is not legal to reproduce, duplicate, or transmit any part of this document in either electronic means or in printed format. Recording of this publication is strictly prohibited and any storage of this document is not allowed unless with written permission from the publisher except for the use of brief quotations in a book review.

This book contains works of fiction. Any resemblance to persons living or dead, or places, events, or locations is purely coincidental.

Table Of Contents

Preface - Message to the Reader 1

Introduction 5

The Psalms of Solomon 10

    Psalm 1 11

    Psalm 2 12

    Psalms Of Salomon 2–4 14

    Psalm 3 15

    Psalm 4 16

    Psalms Of Salomon 4–5 17

    Psalm 5 19

    Psalm 6 21

    Psalm 7 22

    Psalm 8 22

    Psalms Of Salomon 8–9 23

    Psalm 9 26

    Psalm 10 28

    Psalm 11 29

- Psalms Of Salomon 11–14 29
- Psalm 13 29
- Psalm 12 30
- Psalms Of Salomon 14–16 33
- Psalm 16 35
- Psalms Of Salomon 16–17 37
- Psalm 17 37
- Psalms Of Salomon 17–18 40
- Psalm 18 42
- Psalms Of Salomon 18 42

Thank You for Reading 44

Preface - Message to the Reader

What If You Could Help Rebuild the Greatest Library in Human History?

Thousands of years ago, the Library of Alexandria stood as the crown jewel of human achievement — a sanctuary where the collected wisdom of every known civilization was gathered, preserved, and shared freely.

And then, it was lost.

Through fire, conquest, and the slow erosion of time, humanity lost not just books — but ideas, dreams, discoveries, and stories that could have changed the world forever.

Today, the Library of Alexandria lives again — and you are invited to be a part of its restoration.

Our mission is simple yet profound:

To rebuild the greatest library the world has ever known, and to translate all timeless works into every language and dialect, so that no seeker of knowledge is ever left behind again.

By joining our movement to rebuild the modern Library of Alexandria, you become part of an unprecedented mission:

- **Unlimited Access to the Greatest Audiobooks & eBooks Ever Written:**

    Instantly explore thousands of legendary works—Plato, Shakespeare, Jane Austen, Leo Tolstoy, and countless more. All instantly available to read or listen, placing a complete literary universe at your fingertips.

- **Beautiful Paperback & Deluxe Editions at Printing Cost**

    Own any title as an elegant paperback, deluxe hardcover, or stunning collectible boxset—offered to you at true printing cost, delivered straight to your door. Build your personal Library of Alexandria, crafted for beauty, built for durability, and worthy of proud display.

- **Fresh Translations for Modern Readers—in Every Language & Dialect**

    Enjoy timeless masterpieces reimagined in clear, contemporary language—no more outdated phrases or obscure references. Alongside the original versions, we're tirelessly translating these classics into every language and dialect imaginable, ensuring accessibility and understanding across cultures and generations.

- **Join a Global Renaissance of Literature & Knowledge**

   You directly support expanding our library, publishing deluxe editions at true cost, translating works into all global languages, and bringing humanity's greatest stories to people everywhere. By joining today, you're not just preserving a legacy of masterpieces; you set in motion a powerful wave of literary accessibility.

Become a Torchbearer of Knowledge.

Join us for free now at **LibraryofAlexandria.com**

Together, we will ensure that the light of human wisdom never fades again.

With gratitude and a shared love of knowledge,

The Modern Library of Alexandria Team

Visit:

www.libraryofalexandria.com

Or scan the code below:

Introduction

Prayers in Exile: Faith, Repentance, and the Hope for Redemption

The Psalms of Solomon offer one of the most poignant, raw, and spiritually rich glimpses into the heart of Jewish piety during the intertestamental period—the centuries between the writing of the Hebrew Bible and the emergence of the New Testament. Composed likely in the first century BCE by devout Jewish scribes, these eighteen poetic hymns express a wide range of emotional and spiritual responses to the crises of their time: national collapse, foreign occupation, internal corruption, and personal sin. Yet more than a historical document, this text is a living collection of sacred songs that continue to speak across generations to anyone wrestling with injustice, longing for divine deliverance, or striving to remain faithful in the midst of uncertainty.

These psalms were written in a period of great upheaval following the desecration of the Jerusalem Temple, likely in response to the Hasmonean decline and the growing threat of Roman domination. In this historical context, the faithful cried out for a return to holiness and justice. They mourned the sins of their people, lamented the rise of the wicked, and longed for a righteous king from the line of David. But even amid despair, they held fast to their trust in the steadfast love and justice of God.

The Psalms of Solomon are not attributed to King Solomon in the sense of authorship, but evoke his name symbolically—as a figure of wisdom, prayer, and divinely anointed rule. In the voice of these psalms, we hear the echoes of Davidic longing, the wisdom of the sages, and the urgency of the prophets. They combine the literary elegance of the biblical Psalms with the prophetic fervor of books like Isaiah and Jeremiah. And yet, they stand alone in their directness, moral clarity, and unique eschatological hope.

Unlike some of the more ecstatic or mystical texts of the same period, the Psalms of Solomon are grounded in the lived experience of the faithful community. They are deeply ethical, focused on righteousness, repentance, and justice. They express outrage at hypocrisy and corruption among religious leaders, deep grief over exile and suffering, and unwavering hope for a time when God will vindicate the righteous and judge the wicked. In this way, they act both as mirror and lamp: reflecting the spiritual condition of the people, and illuminating the path back to God.

One of the most striking features of this collection is its theology of repentance. These psalms consistently affirm that God is merciful, but that true relationship with Him requires contrition, humility, and obedience. The psalmist speaks not only for the nation but from the soul—offering prayers of personal confession, recommitment, and praise. It is this deeply personal, vulnerable quality that makes these hymns timeless. They do not shy away from the pain of failure or the terror of divine judgment—but they always return to the mercy and sovereignty of God.

These psalms also envision a future redemption. The faithful await a Messiah—not a military conqueror, but a righteous king who will purify Israel and bring peace through justice and divine power. This longing anticipates the later Christian conception of the Messiah while remaining rooted in Jewish national hopes. The text is filled with eschatological expectation—not in the form of apocalypse, but as a sober confidence in the restoration of the faithful and the defeat of evil.

Spiritual Resilience and Poetic Insight for the Modern Soul

For today's readers, The Psalms of Solomon offer both a spiritual balm and a moral compass. They speak to moments of personal and collective crisis with an honesty rarely found in later theological treatises. These are not abstract reflections—they are prayers shaped in the crucible of suffering, written not to explain God but to cry out to Him. They validate the experience of feeling abandoned, betrayed, or overwhelmed, while still lifting the soul toward gratitude, endurance, and trust.

These psalms model how to pray when words fail. When injustice reigns, when leadership falters, when enemies seem to prevail—these sacred songs teach us not to despair, but to turn more deeply to God. They teach us that God sees the heart, that He does not forget His people, and that righteousness will be rewarded. They offer a theology of action: repentance leads to restoration, humility leads to exaltation, and faith in adversity becomes the path to hope.

Their poetic style is also a source of lasting inspiration. The psalmists use repetition, parallelism, vivid imagery, and rhythmic cadences to elevate their words beyond petition into praise. Their structure recalls the biblical Psalms, but their tone is often more direct and impassioned. The language is charged with moral urgency and spiritual intimacy. These are hymns to be read slowly, reflected upon deeply, and returned to often.

This modern translation has been crafted to honor the poetic and spiritual depth of the original while making it accessible for today's readers. Archaic phrasing has been rendered in contemporary language. Symbolism has been retained but clarified where needed. The result is a translation that speaks to both the heart and the mind—inviting the reader not just to learn from the psalms, but to pray with them.

Whether you approach this text as a historical document, a devotional aid, or a source of poetic beauty, you will find in The Psalms of Solomon a faithful companion for your spiritual journey. They will give voice to your gratitude and your grief, your longing and your love. They will challenge you to walk uprightly, to remain steadfast in trials, and to trust in the justice and mercy of God.

May these sacred songs guide your heart to deeper repentance, firmer hope, and more radiant faith. And may the God who inspired them bring you peace in every season of life.

The Psalms of Solomon

This collection of eighteen war songs is a rare treasure from an ancient Semitic writer. Although the original manuscript was lost over time, Greek translations have survived, and a Syriac version was later discovered. In 1909, Dr. Rendel Harris translated this Syriac version into English, allowing people to read these powerful songs once again.

These songs were written around the mid-First Century B.C. Their main focus is on the actions of Pompey in Palestine and his eventual death in Egypt in 48 B.C. The historical background connects these verses to real events from that time.

These psalms were highly valued in the early Church and were shared widely among believers. They appear in different ancient texts and historical records from the first few centuries of Christianity. However, for reasons that remain unclear, they eventually stopped being used and were forgotten. After many centuries, they have been rediscovered and made available once more.

Besides their historical importance, these songs also stand out for their poetic beauty. Their words flow with the rhythm of battle, like the sound of trumpets, stirring the emotions of the reader. The psalms paint a vivid picture of ancient history, as if written by someone who witnessed the events firsthand.

The verses describe Pompey as he comes from the West, leaving destruction behind him. He uses battering rams to tear down city walls, defiles the temple altar, and is ultimately killed in Egypt after a violent and ruthless campaign. In these songs, the "righteous" seem to represent the Pharisees, while the "sinners" may symbolize the Sadducees. These psalms are more than just poetry—they tell the dramatic story of a people struggling to survive in the midst of chaos and war.

Psalm 1

I cried out to the Lord when I was overwhelmed with trouble, calling on God when sinners rose against me. Suddenly, the sounds of war surrounded me, but He heard me because I tried to live righteously.

In my heart, I believed I was righteous, for I had been blessed with success and many children. Their wealth and status spread far and wide, and their glory seemed to reach the heavens.

But in their pride, they believed they could never fall. As they grew richer, they became arrogant. They stopped bringing offerings to God and hid their sins from me, keeping them secret.

Their wrongdoing became worse than those who came before them, and they dishonored the Lord's sacred place with their corruption.

Psalm 2

A psalm about Solomon and Jerusalem.

When the wicked became proud, they used battering rams to break down the strong walls, and You, Lord, did not stop them. Foreign nations invaded Your altar, stepping on it with arrogance. The people of Jerusalem had already defiled Your holy place, dishonoring Your sacred gifts with their sinful actions.

Because of this, You said, "Send them far from Me; I take no joy in them." The beauty of Jerusalem no longer pleased You, and her honor was completely destroyed. Her sons and daughters were taken away as captives, wearing the shame of slavery among the nations.

You judged them for their sins, handing them over to their enemies. You turned away from them and showed no mercy, letting both young and old suffer because they refused to listen to Your commands. Heaven was filled with sorrow, and the earth trembled, for no people on earth had done such terrible things.

The whole world will come to understand Your

righteous judgments, O God. They humiliated the sons of Jerusalem, treating them with cruelty, while strangers defiled her before the sun even rose. They openly embraced evil and mocked Your law. The daughters of Jerusalem were disgraced, losing their purity in confusion and sin.

My soul aches, and my heart is heavy because of all this. But still, I will praise You, O God, with a heart that seeks righteousness, for Your judgments are always just. You have repaid the wicked for their sins, exposing their wrongdoing to prove Your justice. Their memory has been wiped from the earth, for You, O God, are a fair and righteous judge.

The nations laughed at Jerusalem, crushed her underfoot, and stripped away her beauty. She traded her fine clothes for rags, and her crown was replaced with a rope. The glorious headdress You gave her was thrown aside, and her splendor was covered in shame.

Seeing this, I cried out to You, Lord, and pleaded:

"Hasn't Jerusalem suffered enough under Your judgment? You have allowed the nations to mock and destroy her without mercy. Put an end to their fury before they wipe her out completely. You alone, Lord, can bring her back from this ruin."

Translated by Tim Zengerink

Psalms Of Salomon 2–4

Punish them in Your anger, O Lord, for they did not act out of devotion to You but out of selfish greed. They unleashed their fury on us through violence and theft. Do not wait, O God—make them suffer the consequences of their own actions. Expose their arrogance and bring down the prideful enemy.

It did not take long before God revealed their foolishness. In the mountains of Egypt, he was struck down, becoming more despised than the lowest among both land and sea. His body was tossed on the waves in disgrace, with no one to bury him, for God had rejected him in shame.

He forgot that he was just a man and never considered what would come after this life. He proudly declared, "I will rule over the earth and the sea," but he did not realize that God alone is great and powerful. The Lord is the true King of heaven, the One who judges rulers and authorities.

God lifts up the humble and brings down the arrogant, casting them into eternal disgrace because they refused to acknowledge Him. Now, let all the leaders of the earth see the Lord's justice, for He is a righteous King who rules over everything under the heavens.

Praise the Lord, all who honor Him with wisdom, for He shows mercy to those who fear Him and live righteously. He separates the righteous from the wicked, punishing sinners for their actions while showing kindness to the faithful.

The Lord saves those who trust in Him from the shame brought by the wicked and repays sinners for the harm they have done to His people.

The Lord is good to those who call on Him with faith, treating His followers with love and keeping them safe in His strength.

Blessed is the Lord forever, worshiped and praised by His servants.

Psalm 3

Why do you sleep, my soul, and forget to praise the Lord? Sing a new song to God, for He is worthy of all honor. Wake up and play music for Him with all your heart, for a joyful song comes from a heart that loves Him.

The righteous always remember the Lord, giving thanks and trusting in His justice. They do not resist His discipline because they know He is always good. Even when they face struggles, they do not blame Him but wait patiently for His help. They keep their eyes on Him, knowing He is their salvation.

Their righteousness comes from their Savior, and sin does not take hold in their homes. They carefully examine their lives, making sure to remove anything that leads them away from God. Through fasting and humbling themselves, they seek forgiveness for sins they did not realize they committed. The Lord purifies the hearts of those who are devoted to Him and blesses their homes.

But sinners curse their lives, their birth, and even the pain their mothers went through to bring them into the world. They continue in their sin, going deeper into evil without any hope of turning back. Their destruction will last forever, and they will be forgotten by the righteous.

This is the destiny of sinners, but those who fear the Lord will have eternal life. The light of the Lord will shine on them, and they will live with Him forever, never to be separated from His presence.

Psalm 4

Why do you, someone who disrespects the holy, sit among the faithful while your heart is far from the Lord?

You anger the God of Israel with your sinful actions.

You speak proudly, acting as if you are better than

everyone else.

You judge harshly but are quick to condemn others for their sins.

Psalms Of Salomon 4–5

You strike first as if you are passionate for righteousness, but you are guilty of many sins and selfish pleasures.

Your eyes wander to every woman without care, and your words are full of lies when you make promises.

At night, when no one is watching, you sin as if you cannot be seen. You use secret signals to tempt women and enter homes pretending to be innocent.

May God remove such hypocrites from among His faithful people—those who live in corruption and selfishness.

May God expose their actions, showing their lies and shame. Let the faithful praise God's justice when sinners are removed from the righteous.

A people-pleaser twists the law for his own gain, setting his sights on the home of a good man, like a serpent waiting to destroy wisdom with clever words.

He lies to get what he wants, leaving innocent people helpless.

He ruins families with his sinful actions, deceiving

others while thinking no one will see or judge him.

Filled with wickedness, he goes from house to house, spreading chaos with his words.

Like the grave, he is never satisfied. O Lord, let him face disgrace before You.

May his days be filled with suffering, and his nights with restless sorrow.

May his work fail, and his home be left empty.

Let him grow old in loneliness, without children, until the end of his life.

May his body be left for wild animals to devour, and may the bones of sinners lie in disgrace under the sun.

May ravens pluck out the eyes of those who destroy families, chasing after their own desires.

They have forgotten You, O God, and have no fear of You.

They have angered and provoked You.

Remove them from the earth, for they have deceived the innocent with false kindness.

Blessed are those who fear the Lord with pure hearts.

The Lord will rescue them from liars and sinners and protect them from the traps of the wicked.

May God remove the arrogant who do wrong, for He is a great and powerful judge who rules with justice.

Let Your mercy, O Lord, be upon all who love You.

Psalm 5

A psalm of Solomon.

O Lord God, I will gladly praise Your name among those who know Your just and fair judgments.

You are kind and full of mercy, a safe place for the poor. When I call out to You, please do not ignore me.

No one can take anything from a strong man unless You allow it, Lord. Everything, including people and what they have, is measured by You. No one can receive more than what You have decided.

When we are in trouble, we call on You, O God, because You are our protector, and Your judgments are always right.

You do not forget the cries of those who suffer or the needs of the poor.

Keep us safe and lead us, O Lord, for Your name is our strong refuge, and Your righteousness lasts forever.

Psalms Of Salomon 5–8

You will not ignore our prayers, for You are our

God, faithful and true. Do not let Your hand be too heavy on us, or in our suffering, we may turn to sin. If You bring us back to You, we will not wander far but will return with open and willing hearts.

If I am hungry, I will cry out to You, O God, and You will provide for me. You take care of the birds in the sky and the fish in the sea. You send rain to dry lands, making grass grow for all living things. You feed wild animals and provide for every creature that depends on You.

You sustain kings, rulers, and entire nations, O Lord. Who else can the poor and needy turn to except You, their God? You hear them, for You are kind and forgiving. You bring joy to the humble and show mercy to all who seek You.

People often give with hesitation, delaying their kindness for another day. Even when they help without complaint, true generosity is rare. But Your blessings, Lord, are rich and overflowing, given freely to those who put their trust in You.

Your mercy covers the whole earth, O Lord, and Your kindness reaches all of creation. Blessed is the one whom You remember and provide for, giving them exactly what they need. Too much leads to sin, but true happiness comes from having just enough, along with righteousness.

This is where Your favor is found—a life filled with goodness and justice. May those who fear the Lord rejoice in His kindness, and may Your love rest upon Israel in Your kingdom.

Blessed is the glory of the Lord, for He is our King.

Psalm 6

In Hope. A Psalm of Solomon.

Blessed is the one whose heart is always ready to call on the name of the Lord. When they remember Him, salvation is near. The Lord guides their steps and protects the work of their hands.

They will not be troubled by bad dreams or afraid when crossing rivers or facing stormy seas. When they wake up, they praise the name of the Lord. With a strong and faithful heart, they sing songs of worship to their God.

They pray to the Lord for their family, and He listens to all who respect and honor Him. He fulfills the desires of those who place their hope in Him.

Blessed is the Lord, who shows mercy to those who truly love Him.

Psalm 7

A Psalm of Solomon. A Prayer for Restoration.

Do not leave us, O God, or our enemies will rise against us. You have already rejected them—do not let them trample the land You have given to Your people.

Correct us, O Lord, as You see fit, but do not hand us over to other nations. Even if You allow death to come, it will only happen by Your command, for You are merciful and will not stay angry forever.

As long as Your name is with us, we will find mercy, and no nation will be able to defeat us. You are our shield and protector. When we call on You, You hear us.

Your love for Israel never ends. You will never abandon Your people. We remain under Your care, shaped by Your correction and guided by Your wisdom.

When the time comes for You to rescue us, You will show mercy to the house of Jacob, keeping the promises You made.

Psalm 8

A Psalm of Solomon. A Song of Victory.

I heard the sounds of trouble—the noise of war.

Trumpets blasted, warning of violence and destruction.

The cries of many people roared like a powerful wind, like a storm sweeping through the land, burning everything in its path.

In my heart, I wondered, "Where will God bring justice for all this?"

Psalms Of Salomon 8–9

I heard a cry from Jerusalem, the city of God's holy temple. The news crushed my spirit—I trembled, my knees felt weak, and my heart filled with fear. My whole body shook as if my bones were breaking. I thought to myself, "Surely, they will turn back to God and follow His ways."

I reflected on God's judgments, which have been in place since the creation of heaven and earth, and I recognized the fairness of His eternal decisions. God revealed their sins in the open, in the bright light of day. All the earth witnessed His righteous justice.

Yet in secret places, deep in the shadows, they committed terrible sins, breaking God's law without shame. Sons slept with their mothers, fathers with their daughters. Men broke sacred vows, committing adultery with their neighbors' wives. They swore oaths to protect each other in their wickedness.

They stole from God's sanctuary as if there was no one to stop them. They defiled His altar with impurity, treating holy sacrifices as worthless, even desecrating them with blood. They committed every kind of sin, surpassing even the nations in their corruption.

In response, God sent confusion upon them. He gave them over to their sins like drunkards lost in their own wickedness. From distant lands, He brought a powerful enemy who waged war against Jerusalem and its people.

The leaders of the city welcomed this enemy with joy, saying, "Come in peace; we welcome you to our land." They made the roads smooth for his arrival, opened Jerusalem's gates, and decorated the city as if preparing for a celebration.

But he did not come in peace. He entered like a conqueror, walking through the streets with pride and power. He seized Jerusalem's towers and broke through its walls, for God had allowed it while the people continued in their disobedience.

He slaughtered their rulers and silenced their wise men. The blood of Jerusalem flowed like polluted water. He captured their sons and daughters—children born in sin—and took them into captivity.

Still, they continued in their wicked ways, just as their ancestors had done. They desecrated Jerusalem and defiled everything that had been set apart for God's name. Yet through all this, God's judgment remained just, for He is holy and righteous.

The faithful, innocent like lambs, stood in the midst of these punishments. Blessed is the Lord, who judges the earth with fairness. "We have seen Your justice, O God. We have witnessed Your truth with our own eyes."

We honor Your name, lifted high forever, for You are the God of righteousness. You discipline Israel with justice. Show us mercy once again, O God. Gather the scattered people of Israel with kindness and love, for Your faithfulness never fails.

Though we have been stubborn, You are the One who corrects us. Do not leave us, O God, or the nations will destroy us as if we had no Savior. You have been our God from the beginning, and You are still our hope, O Lord.

We will not turn away from You, for Your judgments are fair and merciful. Your goodness remains with us and our children forever.

O Lord, our Savior, we will never be shaken again.

Blessed and praised is the Lord for His righteous judgments, spoken by the mouths of the faithful.

And blessed is Israel, forever secure in the Lord.

Psalm 9

A Psalm of Solomon. A Call to Repentance.

When Israel was taken away to a foreign land and turned from the Lord who had saved them, they lost the inheritance He had given them. They were forced to leave, separated from the land of their ancestors.

In exile, they remembered God's correction, feeling the heavy weight of their sins. They mourned their distance from His promises and cried out for Him to restore them.

But even in their punishment, the Lord remained merciful, for He is a faithful and righteous God.

Psalms Of Salomon 9–11

The people of Israel were scattered among the nations, fulfilling God's word, so that Your justice, O Lord, would be proven right in the face of our sins. You are a fair judge over all the earth, and Your judgments will never change.

No act of injustice is hidden from You. You see everything Your faithful servants do, O Lord. No one can hide from Your knowledge, O God.

Each person chooses their own path—whether to

follow righteousness or to walk in sin. In Your fairness, You hold everyone accountable and judge them by their actions.

Those who live righteously store up life in Your presence, but those who live in wickedness bring destruction upon themselves. Your judgments are always right, applying to every person and every family.

Who will receive Your kindness, O God, if not those who call on You with honest hearts? You wash away sin for those who admit their wrongs and seek forgiveness. Shame weighs heavy on us, O Lord, and we bow our heads in regret for all we have done.

Who else will You forgive but those who humbly confess their sins? You bless the righteous and do not turn away from them because of past mistakes. You show kindness even to sinners who repent and return to You.

Now, You are our God, and we are the people You have loved and chosen. Look upon us with mercy, O God of Israel, for we belong to You. Do not take Your kindness away from us, or our enemies will defeat us.

You chose the descendants of Abraham above all nations and placed Your name upon us, O Lord. You will not abandon us forever. You made a promise to our ancestors on our behalf, and we trust that You will restore us when we turn back to You.

The Lord's mercy lasts forever over the house of Israel, keeping us through every generation.

Psalm 10

A Hymn of Solomon.

Blessed is the one whom the Lord remembers and corrects, guiding them away from the path of sin. His discipline helps cleanse them so that sin does not take over their life.

Those who humbly accept correction will be made pure, for the Lord is kind to those who endure His teaching. He keeps the righteous on the right path and does not let them go astray.

The Lord's mercy is with those who truly love Him. He remembers His servants with compassion, for His truth is written in His everlasting law. His covenant stands as a testimony to His ways and His care for humanity.

Our God is righteous and faithful in all His judgments, forever. Let Israel lift its voice in praise and rejoice in the name of the Lord.

The faithful will speak of His goodness among the people, and the Lord will show mercy to the poor, bringing joy to the hearts of Israel.

For God is kind and full of mercy, and His love lasts

for all time. Let the people of Israel praise His name, for His salvation brings eternal joy to His people.

Psalm 11

A Psalm of Solomon. A Call to Hope.

Blow the trumpet in Zion, calling the holy ones together. Announce the good news in Jerusalem, for the God of Israel has shown His mercy and come to His people.

Stand on the heights, O Jerusalem, and see your children returning, gathered once more by the Lord.

From the east and the west, they come back to You, O Lord, rejoicing in their God.

From the north and the farthest islands, God has brought them home, uniting them through His mercy and power.

Psalms Of Salomon 11–14

The Lord has made the high mountains level and the hills smooth, clearing a path for His people.

Psalm 13

The forests provided shade as they passed, and God made fragrant trees grow along their path. This was so that Israel could walk through and see the glorious presence of their God.

Jerusalem, dress yourself in glory and put on the robe of holiness, for God has spoken everlasting blessings over Israel.

May the Lord keep His promises to Israel and Jerusalem. May He lift up His people by the power of His glorious name, for His mercy and love will always remain with Israel.

Psalm 12

A Psalm of Solomon. A Prayer Against the Words of the Wicked.

O Lord, save me from the wicked and lawless,

from those who speak lies and spread slander.

The words of the corrupt are twisted and destructive,

like a fire that burns through a city, leaving it in ruins.

He spreads falsehoods to destroy homes,

tearing down joy and bringing chaos with his lies.

He stirs up conflict and turns people against each other, using his deceitful words to bring division into peaceful places.

O God, protect the innocent from the harm of these evildoers.

Scatter the bones of the slanderers far away,

far from those who honor You.

Let every lying tongue be silenced in the fire of judgment,

far from the faithful who love You.

Watch over those who seek peace and justice,

and guide those who build harmony in their homes.

The Lord's salvation is upon His servant Israel forever.

Let the sinners be removed from His presence,

and let the faithful receive His promises,

for His mercy endures for those who remain strong in faith.

The Lord's right hand has shielded me,

protecting us from destruction.

His mighty power saved us from the sword,

from hunger, and from death that waits for the wicked.

Fierce beasts rose up against them,

tearing their flesh with sharp teeth,

crushing their bones with mighty jaws.

But the Lord rescued us from every danger.

The faithful feel sorrow over their own sins,

fearing they might be caught in the fate of the wicked.

But the judgment upon sinners is terrible,

and it will not come near the righteous.

The discipline of the faithful is different from the punishment of sinners.

God corrects His people with care,

so the wicked cannot mock or take joy in their struggles.

He rebukes the righteous as a loving father corrects his child,

guiding them as one would a firstborn.

The Lord spares His faithful ones,

cleansing their wrongs through His discipline.

The righteous will live forever,

but sinners will face destruction,

and their names will be forgotten.

The Lord's mercy is endless for those who follow Him,

and His compassion is upon those who fear Him.

God is faithful to those who love Him sincerely,

to those who accept His correction with patience.

He blesses those who walk in righteousness,

following His commands that lead to life.

The faithful will live by His words forever,

like trees in His garden, bearing fruit that never fades.

Their roots are deep and strong,

never to be uprooted as long as the heavens endure.

The Lord cares for His faithful ones,

and His promises stand as their unshakable foundation.

All who walk in His ways will thrive in His light,

living by the law of life He has given to His people.

Psalms Of Salomon 14–16

God's chosen people, Israel, are His special inheritance, the ones He loves. But this is not true for those who sin and reject His laws. They chase after temporary pleasures and embrace wrongdoing. They focus on their own desires and forget about God and His ways.

Translated by Tim Zengerink

God sees everything about every person, even the hidden thoughts of the heart before they form. Because of this, sinners will inherit darkness, destruction, and eternal separation from Him. On the day when God shows mercy and favor to the righteous, sinners will not stand, for their own actions have sealed their fate.

But those who love the Lord and follow His ways will receive eternal life, and their joy will never end.

When I was struggling and felt hopeless, I called on the name of the Lord. I placed my trust in the God of Jacob, and He saved me.

For You, O God, are a safe place and a source of hope for the humble and the poor. Who is truly strong, O Lord, except the one who trusts in You completely? And what power does anyone have except in praising Your name?

With songs of joy and hearts full of gratitude, we lift up our voices to You. These praises come from a faithful and righteous heart, the first and best offerings of thankfulness to You. Those who live this way will not be shaken by evil. The fire of judgment will not touch them.

When Your anger falls upon sinners, O Lord, everything they own will be destroyed. But Your protection is upon the righteous, keeping them safe. Famine, war, and death will not come near them, for trouble will flee from them as if chased away.

Sinners, however, will not escape Your judgment, Lord. They will be overtaken by destruction, for they have been marked for ruin. Their inheritance is darkness, suffering, and despair. The wrong they have done will follow them even after death.

Their wealth and possessions will not last, and their children will not inherit anything from them, for their sins will destroy everything they leave behind.

On the day of the Lord's judgment, when God brings justice to the earth, sinners will be wiped out forever. They will face the full weight of His righteous anger.

But those who fear the Lord, who respect and love Him, will receive mercy on that day. They will be saved by His kindness and grace.

However, the unrepentant and rebellious sinners will be destroyed forever, never to rise again.

Psalm 16

A Hymn of Solomon. A Prayer For Help.

When my soul drifted away and fell into deep sleep, I stumbled, lost like those who live without God. For a moment, I felt myself slipping toward death, nearing the gates of the grave alongside sinners.

But even when I felt distant from the God of Israel, His endless mercy saved me. He reached out, waking me like a rider prods a horse to move, stirring me to return to Him. He has always been my Savior and Protector, rescuing me when I was weak.

I will praise You, O God, with a thankful heart, for You lifted me up and gave me salvation. You did not let me be counted among those destined for destruction.

Do not take Your mercy from me, O God. Let me always remember You, even to my last breath. Rule over my heart, Lord, and protect me from sin and every temptation that leads people astray.

Do not let me be deceived by the beauty of someone who disrespects Your law or by anything that tempts me to sin. Guide the work of my hands so that I may serve You, and lead my steps so I always walk in Your ways.

Keep my mouth and lips pure, so that only words of truth come from me. Remove all anger and reckless wrath from my heart, so they do not lead me into sin. Help me not to complain or lose faith when I go through hardship.

Lord, keep me strong in faith and truth. Let Your guidance and mercy be the light that leads me, keeping me close to You always.

Psalms Of Salomon 16–17

When I sin, You correct me to bring me back to the right path, Lord. Your discipline has a purpose—it is how You restore me.

Fill my heart with strength and joy, for when You support me, everything You provide is enough. Without Your help, who could handle the weight of discipline, especially during times of struggle and hardship?

When a person is corrected while caught in sin, Your testing often comes through challenges in life and the struggles of poverty. But if the righteous stay strong through these trials, they will find Your kindness and mercy, O Lord.

Psalm 17

A Psalm of Solomon. A Song About the King.

O Lord, You are our King forever. In You, O God, we find our confidence and strength.

Life on earth is short, measured by the days we live and the hope we place in You. But we will trust in You completely, our Savior. Your power lasts forever, full of mercy, and Your kingdom rules with justice over all nations for all time.

You, O Lord, chose David to be king over Israel

and promised him that his descendants would always have a place before You. But because of our sins, enemies rose against us. They attacked and drove us out, though You never gave them that right. They took what did not belong to them and refused to honor Your holy name.

In their arrogance, they built great palaces, thinking they could change what You had set in place. They disrespected David's throne, acting as if they could undo Your will. But You, O God, will bring them down. You will erase their descendants from the earth when You raise up a new ruler, one unlike them. You will punish them for their sins, making sure they face the consequences of their actions.

You showed them no mercy. You wiped out their descendants so none could escape Your judgment. O Lord, You are faithful and just in all Your judgments across the earth.

The wicked destroyed our land, leaving it barren and empty. They killed both the young and the old, showing no mercy—not even to children. In Your anger, You drove them to the west. The rulers of the land were mocked and not spared. The enemy, though an outsider, was proud and had no fear of You, O God.

In Jerusalem, he behaved as the nations do in their own fortified cities. But even among those who were supposed to be faithful, no one showed mercy or upheld the truth. Those who once loved gathering to worship You fled like birds leaving their nests. They wandered in the wilderness to escape evil, and their survival was a sign to those who watched from afar.

The wicked scattered them across the earth. The heavens held back the rain, and the underground springs stopped flowing. The highest mountains became dry because righteousness and justice were nowhere to be found. From kings to common people, all had fallen into sin. The rulers broke Your law, the judges disobeyed, and the people followed in their wickedness.

O Lord, look upon Your people and rise up for them. Send their king, the son of David, at the time You have chosen. Let him rule over Israel, Your servant. Give him strength to break the power of corrupt rulers, cleanse Jerusalem from those who destroy her, and lead with wisdom and justice. Let him drive sinners out of the land You have given to Your people.

Let him crush the pride of the wicked like clay in a potter's hands and destroy their wealth with an iron rod.

Let him defeat sinful nations with the words of his mouth. At his command, may his enemies scatter, and sinners tremble with guilt even in their own hearts. He will gather a holy people and lead them in righteousness.

Translated by Tim Zengerink

Psalms Of Salomon 17–18

He will rule over the tribes of God's people, the ones made holy þy the Lord. He will not allow injustice to remain among them, and no one who does evil will live among them. He will know them well, understanding that they are all God's children.

He will give them their inheritance, dividing the land among the tribes. No outsider will live among them anymore. With wisdom and fairness, he will judge both his own people and the nations.

He will bring the nations under his rule, placing them under his authority. He will bring glory to the Lord across the earth, making Jerusalem holy again and restoring its purity. People from all over the world will come to see his greatness. They will bring gifts and return the scattered sons of Jerusalem. They will witness the shining glory that God has placed upon His city.

He will be a just and righteous king, taught by God Himself. During his reign, there will be no injustice among his people, for all will live in holiness, and he will be the Lord's chosen leader. He will not rely on horses, warriors, or weapons. He will not gather gold and silver for war or trust in a large army to win battles.

Instead, the Lord will be his King and his source of strength, as he places all his hope in God. He will show mercy to every nation that respects him. With the power of his words, he will bring justice to the earth and bless God's people with wisdom and joy. He will live free from sin so that he can lead his people, correct rulers, and remove the wicked with the truth of his words.

He will not waver, always depending on his God. The Lord will fill him with strength through the Holy Spirit, giving him wisdom, understanding, guidance, and righteousness. God's blessing will be with him in everything he does. His trust will be firmly in the Lord, and no one will be able to defeat him.

His actions will be great, and his reverence for God will make him strong. He will lead God's people with fairness and care, making sure that no one is left behind or forgotten. He will guide them with justice, ensuring that no one is treated unfairly or oppressed.

This is the greatness of the king of Israel—the one God has chosen and prepared to rule His people and lead them with discipline and wisdom. His words will be more valuable than the finest gold, more precious than the purest treasures. Among the people, he will judge with wisdom, and his words will be honored as holy among God's chosen ones.

Blessed are those who will live in that time and witness the goodness of Israel, as God restores His people and unites the tribes once again.

May the Lord quickly show mercy to Israel and free His people from those who have defiled them.

The Lord Himself will always be our King, reigning forever.

Psalm 18

God, Your kindness lasts forever in everything You have made. You pour out Your goodness on Israel like a precious gift. When You look at them with love, no one is left in need. You always listen to the cries of the poor who trust in You.

Your justice reaches across the whole earth, but it is full of mercy. Your love stays strong for the descendants of Abraham, the children of Israel, whom You have chosen. Like a caring parent, You guide us with discipline, treating us like a beloved firstborn child, correcting us and leading us away from foolishness.

May God make Israel pure, preparing them for the time of His kindness. May He bless them richly and cover them with His grace.

Psalms Of Salomon 18

On the day God chooses, when He sends His anointed one, blessed are those who will see it. Lucky are those who will witness God's goodness and the amazing things He will do for future generations. Under the leadership and guidance of God's chosen one, people will honor and respect their Lord, living with wisdom, justice, and strength.

This anointed leader will teach everyone to do what is right and help them grow in their respect for God. He will lead them to stand firmly before the Lord, creating a generation devoted to holiness during a time of God's mercy.

Pause and reflect with the sound of music. Our God is great, lifted high above all things. He set the stars and planets in motion, marking the seasons and keeping track of time. These lights in the sky have never strayed from the paths He gave them.

From the moment God created them, they have followed His will. For countless generations, they have remained steady in their course, only changing direction when He commands, passing His instructions through His faithful servants.

Thank You for Reading

Dear Reader,

We hope this timeless classic has sparked your imagination and enriched your literary journey. Now that you've turned the final page, we want to share a vision for the future of reading—one where every classic you've ever wanted to explore is at your fingertips, in a format that best suits your life.

We'd like to invite you to gain immediate, unlimited digital & audiobook access to hundreds of the most treasured literary classics ever written—along with the option to secure deluxe paperback, hardcover & box set editions at printing cost. Together, we can spark a new global literary renaissance alongside our small, independent publishing house called "The Library of Alexandria."

Thousands of years ago, the Library of Alexandria stood as a beacon of knowledge—until it was lost to history. We aim to reignite that spirit of preservation and discovery right now, in the modern age—only this time, it's accessible to all, in every language and every format.

Picture a world where every timeless classic, novel, poem, or philosophical treatise is not only available to read but also updated for today's readers—modernized, translated into any language or dialect, and ready to enjoy in any format you choose, whether that is in an eBook, audiobook, paperback, or deluxe hardcover & box set version a printing cost.

By joining our movement to rebuild the modern Library of Alexandria, you become part of an unprecedented mission to offer:

- **Unlimited Audiobook & eBook Access to the Greatest Classics of All Time**

    Instantly explore thousands of legendary works, from Plato and Shakespeare to Jane Austen and Leo Tolstoy. All are instantly ready to read or listen to, giving you a complete literary universe at your fingertips.

- **Paperback & Deluxe Editions at Printing Costs:**

    Purchase any title in a paperback, deluxe hardbound, or deluxe boxset edition at printing costs, shipped right to your doorstep. Curate your personal library of Alexandria with editions worthy of display—crafted to last, designed to captivate, and delivered straight to your door.

- **Modern translations for Contemporary Readers in all languages and dialects**

    Discover a vast selection of classics reimagined in clear, current language—no more struggling with outdated phrases or obscure references. Next to the original versions, we aim to offer translations in as many languages and dialects as possible.

    As we continue our translation efforts and add new languages, readers everywhere can connect with these works as if they were written today. By bridging linguistic divides, you're contributing to ensuring that these timeless stories become more meaningful, accessible, and inspiring for people across the globe.

- **Your Personal Library of Alexandria:**

    Over the months and years, you'll curate a unique physical archive of classics—each volume a testament to your taste, curiosity, and love of knowledge. It's not just about owning books—it's about curating a cultural legacy you'll cherish and pass down for generations to come.

- **Join a Global Literary Renaissance:**

    Your support fuels an ongoing mission: allowing us to reinvest in offering deluxe print editions (including special boxsets) at their true cost, broaden the range of available formats and translations, and extend the reach of these works to new audiences worldwide. By joining today, you're not just preserving a legacy of masterpieces; you set in motion a powerful wave of literary accessibility.

We are more than a publisher—we're a movement, and we can't do it alone. Your support lets us scale our mission, preserving and reimagining history's greatest works for tomorrow's readers.

Become a Torchbearer of knowledge.

Thank you for picking up this book and allowing us into your literary journey. As you turn the pages, know that you're part of something larger: a global effort to keep these stories alive, share their wisdom across borders and generations, and spark a true cultural revival for the modern era.

If this resonates with you—please consider taking the next step by visiting:

www.libraryofalexandria.com

With gratitude and a shared love of knowledge,

The Modern Library of Alexandria Team

Visit:

www.libraryofalexandria.com

Or scan the code below:

www.ingramcontent.com/pod-product-compliance
Lightning Source LLC
LaVergne TN
LVHW030631080426
835512LV00021B/3460